which wine is in your glass?

UNDERSTANDING & ENJOYING WINE

CHRIS LOSH

RYLAND
PETERS
& SMALL

LONDON NEW YORK

SENIOR DESIGNER Anna Murphy
SENIOR EDITOR Clare Double
PRODUCTION MANAGER Patricia Harrington
PICTURE RESEARCH Emily Westlake
ART DIRECTOR Gabriella Le Grazie
PUBLISHING DIRECTOR Alison Starling

First published in the United Kingdom in 2005
by Ryland Peters & Small
20–21 Jockey's Fields
London WC1R 4BW
www.rylandpeters.com

10 9 8 7 6 5 4 3 2 1

ISBN 1 84172 915 9

A catalogue record for this book is available
from the British Library.

Printed in China

contents

introduction

LET'S JUST GET ONE THING STRAIGHT FROM THE OUTSET. THERE'S NO ROOM IN THIS BOOK FOR WINE SNOBBERY. WINE SNOBS ARE ALL ABOUT TELLING PEOPLE WHAT NOT TO DRINK, ABOUT WRITING OFF WHOLE COUNTRIES AND ABOUT DISMISSING OTHER PEOPLE'S PERSONAL TASTE BECAUSE IT DOESN'T COINCIDE WITH THEIR OWN.

But the spirit of wine is the opposite of all these things. It's about 'do drink', not 'don't drink'; about discovering new things, not reinforcing old prejudices; about empowering, not belittling.

In fact, for me, there's only one real 'wine crime', and that's drinking the same bottle week in, week out – it's such a waste, when there's so much fantastic stuff out there now to choose from.

Red wines, white wines, rosé wines and pricey wines. Sweet, dry, fortified and fizzy, from the deserts of Australia to the foothills of the Andes, from Napa Valley to northern France.

The whole world, it seems, is making wine. Why? Because it's the best drink on the planet, that's why.

And they're not just making wines with the same old grapes, oh no. As new parts of the world come to terms with the likes of Cabernet Sauvignon and Chardonnay, so they've started to turn their attention to new grape varieties and new areas. Turn your back for a second and somewhere that you thought you understood has changed beyond all recognition.

Maybe it is a slightly mad, chaotic whirl, and maybe it can be a bit intimidating – but boy is it exciting!

There has never been so much different wine on the market – and never before has the quality been so reliably good. I've had plenty of wine over the last few years that was a bit boring or ordinary, but I can't remember the last time I had one that was actually really bad.

All in all, it's no exaggeration to say that we're lucky enough to be living through a golden age for wine;

and this book is designed to help you make the most of it. So put aside your fear, tell the wine snobs to go hang and go out there and get drinking. Cheers!

what affects the flavour?

IN A SENSE, THIS IS ONE OF THOSE 'HOW LONG IS A PIECE OF STRING?' QUESTIONS. SCIENTISTS AND WINEMAKERS WILL ARGUE UNTIL EVERYONE ELSE HAS FALLEN ASLEEP ABOUT HOW MUCH VARIOUS FACTORS INFLUENCE WHAT'S IN YOUR GLASS. BUT WHAT'S CERTAINLY TRUE IS THAT WE CAN PICK OUT HALF A DOZEN AREAS THAT ALL HAVE A MAJOR EFFECT ON WHAT YOUR WINE ACTUALLY TASTES LIKE.

THE GRAPE VARIETY

Just as there are different makes of car, so there are different types of grape, which have different characteristics and flavours. Some like hot places, others cool; some make wine that can age for years, others give bottles that need to be drunk young. 'Dual Varietals' (blends of two grape varieties) are becoming more common.

THE CLIMATE

A grape grown in a hot, or super-sunny, place will taste different from a grape of the same variety grown in a cooler place. Broadly speaking, the wine from the hot area will be fruitier and sweeter with higher alcohol, the one from the cooler area will be less in-your-face and more elegant.

THE SOIL

Yes, really! The character of a wine can alter depending on whether it's grown on sandy soil, clay, granite or limestone. Riesling and Pinot Noir show up these differences most clearly.

THE WINERY

Winemakers like to fiddle with grapes once they've got them in the winery. They ferment them at different temperatures for different times, blend them with other grapes, and put the wine in barrels. Which brings us to...

THE BARRELS

A wine which has been fermented or aged in oak tastes significantly different to one which hasn't. Typically, it'll be 'bigger', with noticeable toasty, spicy aromas – and the longer a wine is left in the barrel, the more pronounced the effect. But putting wine in a barrel doesn't work for every grape variety.

THE VINE AGE/WINE AGE

As in life, age is important in wine. Older vines give less, but more concentrated, fruit than young vines, while a wine that has been left to sit in a bottle for twenty years will taste very different to one that's just six months old. With time, good wines lose their primary fruit flavours and become more subtle and complex, whereas cheap wines just go downhill!

wine styles

famous red wines

CABERNET SAUVIGNON

REGIONS The Médoc villages in Bordeaux: Margaux, St-Estèphe, Pauillac, St-Julien; Napa Valley and Alexander Valley (California); Maipo and Colchagua Valleys (Chile), Stellenbosch (South Africa); Coonawarra and Margaret River (Australia)

PRODUCERS Châteaux Lafite, Latour, Mouton-Rothschild, Margaux, Haut-Brion, Cos d'Estournel, Pichon-Longueville and Lynch-Bages (all Bordeaux's 'left bank'); Screaming Eagle, Opus One, Harlan Estate (California); Almaviva (Chile)

MERLOT

REGIONS Pomerol and St-Émilion (Bordeaux's 'right bank'); Rapel Valley (Chile); Napa and Sonoma Valleys (California)

PRODUCERS Famous Merlot-dominant estates in Bordeaux include Châteaux Pétrus, Pavie, Trotanoy, Lafleur and l'Angélus

SHIRAZ/SYRAH

REGIONS Côte-Rôtie, Hermitage, St-Joseph, Crozes-Hermitage, Cornas (all northern Rhône); Barossa Valley, McLaren Vale (Australia)

PRODUCERS Chapoutier, Chaves, Jaboulet, Guigal (all northern Rhône); Penfolds Grange, Henschke Hill of Grace (Australia); Montes Folly (Chile)

PINOT NOIR

REGIONS Gevrey-Chambertin, Vosne-Romanée, Vougeot, Morey-St-Denis, Chambolle-Musigny, Nuits-St-Georges (all Burgundy); Russian River Valley and Carneros (California); Marlborough and Central Otago (New Zealand)

PRODUCERS Domaine de la Romanée-Conti, Bonneau du Martray, Henri Jayer, Louis Jadot (all Burgundy); Felton Road (Central Otago)

SANGIOVESE

REGIONS Chianti, Montalcino (Italy)

PRODUCERS Villa Cafaggio, Antinori (Chianti); Biondi-Santi (Montalcino)

ZINFANDEL

REGIONS Mendocino and Lodi (California)

PRODUCER Ravenswood (Sonoma Valley)

TEMPRANILLO

REGIONS Rioja and Ribera del Duero (Spain)

PRODUCERS Marques de Riscal and Muga (Rioja), Pesquera de Duero (Ribera del Duero)

MALBEC

REGION Mendoza (Argentina)

PRODUCER Catena

GRENACHE

REGION Châteauneuf-du-Pape (southern Rhône)

PRODUCERS Domaines Perrin and Henri Bonneau

CABERNET SAUVIGNON. IT'S THE WORLD'S MOST-PLANTED QUALITY RED GRAPE VARIETY – THE SECRET BEHIND BOTH SOME OF THE MOST EXPENSIVE RED WINES IN THE WORLD AND A MILLION BOTTLES OF CHEAP AND CHEERFUL PLONK. JUST ABOUT ANYONE WHO'S EVER DRUNK WINE HAS TRIED IT, AND MOST PEOPLE LOVE IT – IT'S THAT KIND OF GRAPE.

cabernet sauvignon

But what makes it so great? Well, at the risk of sounding ridiculously obvious, it's the flavour…

'Cabernet', as it's often known, is capable of delivering a really good, rich, whack of black fruit flavours that stay on your tastebuds long after you've swallowed the dark, brooding liquid in your glass.

Try these classic Cabernet flavours for size: blackcurrants, black cherries, blackberries and plums, chocolate and tobacco, cedars and cassis. Ring any bells? These are big tastes and, if you're looking for an elegant, juicy mouthful of wine, nothing delivers it better than Cabernet.

Of course, with the good there's also some bad. Cabernet is naturally much higher in tannin than most grape varieties, which can make it rather tough to drink. This is particularly true when it's grown in cooler regions or when greedy growers try to wring rather more grapes out of their vines than they should.

'Overcropping' is less of a problem at the top end, where the wines are super-concentrated. But at this level of intensity the tannins can be so fierce

If you're looking for an elegant, juicy mouthful of wine, nothing delivers it better than Cabernet.

that the wines can need years and years of ageing before they settle down a bit and become approachable

This is less the case in places like California, Australia and Chile, where even the top wines are drinkable relatively young. But it's certainly true in Bordeaux, the grape's heartland, where it is often blended with Merlot (see pages 16–17) to flesh it out a bit.

For Bordeaux, Cabernet Central is in the stony, gravelly soils of the Médoc, home to the most famous wine estates in the world. Even if you'll never have the opportunity to drink or buy their wines, the names of Châteaux Lafite, Latour, Mouton-Rothschild, Margaux, Haut-Brion et al carry a special resonance.

SAY THE NAME OUT LOUD, GO ON. SHIRAZ. AS IN
SHIRAZ-MATAZZ, AS IN 'ALL THAT SHIRAZ'. WELL, IT TASTES
LIKE IT SOUNDS: EXOTIC, JAZZY, LIVELY, HEDONISTIC.

shiraz

Actually, Shiraz has two names, since
it's also known in Europe as Syrah
(to rhyme with 'hurrah'). It's fitting, in
a way, because this grape does have
something of a multiple personality,
capable of making wine in a bewildering
array of styles.

Grow it somewhere relatively cool
and it will give you pretty red, raspberry
fruits and distinctly spicy aromas. Stick
it somewhere hot and you get full-on
rich, dark blackberry flavours, overlaid
with chocolate and plums. The Aussies,
meanwhile, have used it to make
fortified wines and even sparkling reds.

But the beauty of Shiraz/Syrah is its
tolerance. It doesn't have ragingly high
tannins or acidity and it gives of its fruit
generously. It's not that there's no such
thing as a bad Shiraz, but you really

have to get it badly wrong both in the vineyard and the winery to make one.

Shiraz, incidentally, is the name of a city in Iran, and popular mythology has it that the grape migrated, over many years, from the Middle East up to France, settling in the Rhône Valley, where it found the steep slopes round the mighty river very much to its liking.

Aussie Shiraz has become a classic wine style, sought after the world over.

You might have heard of the likes of Hermitage and Côte-Rôtie: A-list Syrah areas, both of them, making some of the best wine in France. At the southern end of the Rhône Valley, as it approaches the sea, it's usually blended with other 'Mediterranean grapes' like Grenache and Mourvèdre to give a ripe, spicy mixture.

For all France's pedigree, there are many now who argue that the grape is doing its best work in Australia, where it's been planted for a long, long time and where it seems to like the hot, dry weather. Certainly, Aussie Shiraz has rapidly become a classic wine style, sought after the world over, and is inspiring other New World countries to plant it – with encouraging results.

pinot noir

Get it in the wrong place and you'll never, ever manage to make even a half-decent wine with it. And even in a perfect location, while most grape varieties have a degree of tolerance about them should the weather not go absolutely to plan, prissy Miss Pinot doesn't require much excuse to turn up her roots in a sulk and make something that's beyond simply boring and is actually bad.

And yet, and yet ... when the mood takes Pinot Noir she can give you a wine-drinking experience so sublime as to render you practically speechless – a wine of grace, elegance and understated power that delivers complexity so fine as to be almost weightless. The cherry and strawberry fruit flavours are joined by a host of extraordinary savoury aromas – of leather and leaf-mulch, of farmyards and bitter chocolate – all tied up with the silkiest of tannins.

It's the vinous equivalent of a Mozart piano concerto or Billie Holiday singing 'That Ol' Devil Called Love'; of Olivier playing Hamlet; of Joe Montana throwing a perfect touchdown pass. That is why winemakers continue to put up with her tantrums and turn a blind eye to her idiosyncrasies. Because one year they're sure that everything will go right for them and they will be able to capture that moment of sheer poetry that no other grape can manage.

Part of the difficulty with Pinot Noir is that she is happiest in fairly cool areas; the very ones, in other words, which are most prone to rain and clouds – both of which she hates. Her finest expressions are from Burgundy (all red Burgundy is Pinot Noir), where she changes character enormously, depending on the year, the vineyard and the grower. (Picking good Burgundy is very, very complicated.)

But Pinot Noir is also showing an increased liking for New Zealand's cool South Island (look for Marlborough and Central Otago on the bottle) and cooler areas of California like Russian River Valley, Carneros and the Central Coast. Pinot is a gamble, but get it right and you'll never forget it.

A wine of grace, elegance and understated power that delivers complexity so fine as to be almost weightless.

IF YOU'VE NEVER HEARD OF THIS, DON'T WORRY – THERE'S A GOOD REASON. SANGIOVESE (PRONOUNCED 'SAN-JA-VAYSEY') IS PLANTED ALL OVER ITALY, AND IF YOU'VE EVER DRUNK ITALIAN WINE YOU'VE PROBABLY HAD SOME. YOU JUST WOULDN'T KNOW IT, BECAUSE THE ITALIANS, FOR THE MOST PART, DON'T PUT THE NAME OF THE GRAPE VARIETY ON THE BOTTLE. MEANWHILE, IN COUNTRIES THAT DO BELIEVE IN VARIETAL LABELLING (LIKE AUSTRALIA OR THE US), THIS GRAPE ISN'T WIDELY PLANTED. HENCE ITS MYSTERY STATUS.

sangiovese

What you will probably have heard of, though, is the wine style in which this grape is the main component: Chianti.

Until relatively recently, Chianti was something of a byword for thin, acidic, frankly nasty wines. Producers in

For most wine lovers, Sangiovese reaches its pinnacle when it is mixed with Cabernet Sauvignon.

Tuscany were, for too long, interested only in knocking out large amounts of wine and didn't care much what it tasted like. But that, mercifully, has changed over the last twenty years and at last the grape is starting to show what it is fully capable of.

And what it's capable of is fantastic, mid-weight, cherry-and-plum-flavoured wines with good acidity and tannin. These aren't the sort of wines that

you'll pull the cork from to drink on their own, but with that easy weight and good structure they are fabulous with food.

But for most wine lovers, Sangiovese reaches its pinnacle when it is mixed with Cabernet Sauvignon, which adds weight, silkiness, more depth and a serious ageability to its Sangiovese pal. These so-called Supertuscans are among the best, classiest and most expensive wines in the world.

Talking of the world, the massive Italian diaspora in the early 20th century doesn't seem to have helped spread Sangiovese. Although there are plantings of the grape all over the globe and some producers (especially in California) are making good wine with it, it isn't really planted in any serious numbers. It's probably just a matter of time, though. Keep your eyes peeled.

ZAPPY NAME, ZAPPY KIND OF GRAPE. 'ZIN' HAS BEEN AROUND IN CALIFORNIA SINCE THE 19TH CENTURY AND WHEN IT'S TREATED PROPERLY CAN MAKE SOME OF AMERICA'S BEST AND MOST INDIVIDUAL WINES.

zinfandel

Genetically, it's been traced back to a southern Italian grape called Primitivo, which must have made its way to the New World in the pockets of some far-sighted immigrant. But in California it has taken on a life of its own, giving big, rich, spicy wines of depth and character. It's tolerant, too, and is able to give you a fulfilling glassful from both cooler areas of Sonoma and the broiling Central Valley – though the wines are very different in character.

'White Zinfandel' is the name given to an easy-drinking, sweetish blush (pink) version, made from the same grape. It's OK drunk chilled, but not very exciting.

tempranillo

THIS IS THE CORNERSTONE OF ONE OF THE WORLD'S ABSOLUTELY CLASSIC WINE STYLES: RIOJA. YOU WOULDN'T KNOW IT FROM LOOKING AT THE BOTTLE, THOUGH, BECAUSE VERY FEW LABELS TELL YOU THAT.

It's an easy-going, early-ripening grape (*temprano* is Spanish for 'early' – hence the name), which usually means It's safely in the winery before the worst of the autumn weather arrives. And, under a variety of different regional names, it's planted right across Spain.

Generally speaking, Tempranillo gives a ripe, round, generous dollop of red-fruit flavours (strawberries and plums are common), developing more complexity once It's had a bit of time in oak barrels.

Open and accessible, it drinks well young, so don't be shy to pull the cork.

IF HOLLYWOOD WAS EVER GOING TO MAKE A FILM OF A
GRAPE VARIETY'S LIFE STORY (AND, OK, IT'S UNLIKELY), THEY
WOULD PROBABLY CHOOSE MALBEC. THE STORY BEGINS IN
THE RUSTIC OPEN SPACES OF SOUTH-WEST FRANCE, WHERE
OUR HERO IS BUSY BEING USED IN SMALL AMOUNTS,
BLENDED WITH OTHER GRAPES, RIGHT ACROSS THE REGION.

malbec

His is very much the supporting role,
but he knows he can do better and
hops on a boat to South America,
where after a few false starts he
settles in the vineyards of Argentina.

The locals love him, pamper him
and give him top billing, and before
long he's a star, drunk by presidents
and peasants alike and shipped all
over the world, with his name in big
letters on the bottle.

In Argentina, Malbec is sultry,
perfumed and silky. In Chile, it can
be even darker and more brooding
still, with definite liquorice flavours.
Gotta try it...

grenache

GRENACHE IS ONE OF THE KEY
GRAPES IN PROBABLY THE MOST
DENSELY PLANTED AREA OF VINEYARD
IN THE WORLD, ACROSS THE SOUTH
OF FRANCE AND INTO NORTHERN
SPAIN. SO WHY, YOU MAY WONDER,
ISN'T IT A HOUSEHOLD NAME?

The answer's simple. These areas historically made their wines up of a blend of different grape varieties and didn't bother listing them all on the label. So if you've ever drunk a southern French red (or a Côtes du Rhône) you've probably drunk a wine with a fair bit of Grenache in it and never even realized. If you've ever had a Châteauneuf-du-Pape, then that's just about all Grenache.

The role of Grenache in blended wines is usually one of providing alcohol, which it does very well. But when it's made on its own or allowed to dominate (as in the big, butch monsters from Châteauneuf-du-Pape), you can also savour its cheerful, blowzy big red-fruit and spice flavours. Done well, Grenache is as warming and homely as a log fire.

It hasn't really caught on in the New World for quality wines yet. The Aussies and Californians have used it to make fortified or cheapo jug wine, but this is changing. You may not see it much on its own, but it's ever more likely to form the 'G' part of a 'GSM' compound – Grenache, Shiraz, Mourvèdre.

famous
white wines

CHARDONNAY

REGIONS Puligny-Montrachet, Chassagne-Montrachet, Meursault, Chablis (Burgundy); Russian River Valley, Sonoma Coast, Santa Maria Valley (California); Adelaide Hills, Yarra Valley, Margaret River, Padthaway (Australia)

PRODUCERS Henri Jayer, Comtes Lafon, Coche-Dury, Domaine de la Romanée Conti (Burgundy); Laroche, Raveneau (Chablis); Chain of Ponds, Nepenthe, Cape Mentelle, Yattarna (Australia)

SAUVIGNON BLANC

REGIONS Bordeaux, Sancerre, Pouilly-Fumé (France); Marlborough (New Zealand)

PRODUCERS Henri Bourgeois, Pascal Jolivet (Sancerre); Didier Dagueneau (Pouilly-Fumé); Domaine de Chevalier, Château la Louvière (Bordeaux); Cloudy Bay, Villa Maria (New Zealand)

RIESLING

REGIONS Mosel, Rheingau, Pfalz (Germany); Clare Valley (Australia)

PRODUCERS Müller-Catoir, Dr Loosen, JJ Prüm (Germany); Petaluma (Australia)

GEWÜRZTRAMINER

REGION Alsace (France)

PRODUCERS Trimbach, Zind-Humbrecht, Schoffit

SÉMILLON

REGIONS Bordeaux, Sauternes, Barsac (France); Hunter Valley (Australia)

PRODUCERS Château d'Yquem, Château Suduiraut, Château Climens (Sauternes)

CHENIN BLANC

REGIONS Saumur, Savennières, Vouvray (Loire); Stellenbosch (South Africa)

PRODUCERS Marc Brédif, Domaine Huet (Vouvray)

VIOGNIER

REGION Condrieu (Rhône Valley)

PRODUCER Château Grillet

CHARDONNAY IS THE WINE SUCCESS STORY OF THE LAST TWENTY YEARS; THE WHITE GRAPE VARIETY THAT THE WHOLE WORLD SUDDENLY FELL IN LOVE WITH ALL AT ONCE.

chardonnay

Some people worry that it's become too common, and there is, believe it or not, an unofficial ABC (Anything But Chardonnay) movement. But such people are little more than snobs and killjoys. Chardonnay is popular for a very good reason: it delivers soft, fruity, flavourful wine with attractive pear, melon and apple flavours almost wherever it's grown.

Just look at its geographical spread. It's planted from China to California, on the chilly slopes of northern France and the baking plains of Australia. And in all of these places it manages to turn out wine that may vary in quality and style, and may sometimes be boring but which is nearly always highly drinkable and decent value for money.

One of the good things about Chardonnay (unusual for white wines) is that it likes being fermented or aged

Cheerful and tolerant, Chardonnay is the most good-natured of grapes. It's also capable of greatness.

in oak barrels, which adds attractive spicy, toasty, vanilla and coconut flavours to it. This practice got a little out of hand in the 1990s, with the wines getting too big and oaky. But fortunately now there is a move back away from this and towards a better balance of fruit and oak.

Unlike some grape varieties that are neurotically picky about growing in just the right place, Chardonnay travels with a smile. Cheerful and tolerant, it is the most good-natured of grapes.

It's also capable of greatness. In the limestone soils of Burgundy it makes what for many people are the finest white wines anywhere in the world. That's right, the same grape variety that you bought for £5 to go with your Wednesday-night pasta can disappear into a metaphorical phone booth and come out as Superwine, thanks to Mother Nature and a few diligent growers in northern France.

These wines (unlike most whites) are not necessarily best drunk young, and develop amazing complexity over time. Since Burgundy has a thousand-year head start, it's not surprising that the rest of the world is playing catch-up, but cooler areas of Australia, New Zealand and California show promise.

PART OF THE TROUBLE WITH RIESLING IS THAT IT DOESN'T SOUND SEXY. CHARDONNAY AND SAUVIGNON BLANC HAVE THOSE WONDERFUL SOFT FRENCH VOWEL SOUNDS THAT POSITIVELY DEMAND TO BE ROLLED AROUND THE MOUTH, BUT RIESLING IS KIND OF GERMANIC AND SPIKY.

riesling

And yet it is, probably, the most glorious white grape variety of them all. A hundred years ago, Rieslings from the top German estates were the most expensive wines (not just whites) in the world. People prized them for their ability to age for decades and for their unparalleled complexity. Nowadays, though production is just a large lake compared to the oceans of Sauvignon Blanc and Chardonnay slopping round the world, Riesling is (happily) gaining in popularity once more.

The thing is, Riesling doesn't travel well. You can't just plonk it down in a desert, give it some water and get good wine at the end of it. That's one reason the New World countries have been slower to get the hang of it. Making decent Riesling is all about finding the right place – and that takes time.

So what's it like? Well, if Pinot Noir is a prima donna and Chardonnay an

The best of these wines are a miracle of balance, with softly generous flavours and a whistle-clean finish.

easy-going party grape, Riesling is a reserved intellectual. While it likes things to be dry, it's not a sun-worshipper, preferring it to be sunny well into the autumn rather than broilingly hot over the summer.

The trouble with this is that cool places tend also to be rainy places and,

while you can save Chardonnay, for instance, in a damp year, washed-out Riesling really isn't a great experience.

That's because it is naturally high in acidity. This is a Good Thing, since it allows the wine to age for decades while retaining its freshness, moving from peach and lime flavours to dried fruits and, sometimes, an amazing oiliness quite unlike the flavour profile of any other grape. In years when rain or clouds stop the fruit from ripening nicely, though, you've got problems, with high acidity and no fruit to balance it.

While most Rieslings from New Zealand and Australia are dry, a lot of the classic German Rieslings are just off-dry (or, sometimes, actually sweet). But that doesn't at all mean that they're cloying on the palate. The best of these wines are a miracle of balance, with softly generous flavours and a whistle-clean finish. They work brilliantly with spicy Asian or fusion food and, with lower alcohol, they're good at lunchtimes, too.

NOW, THE FACT THAT YOU'VE NEVER HEARD OF IT DOESN'T NECESSARILY MEAN YOU'VE NEVER DRUNK IT. IF YOU'VE EVER HAD A WHITE BORDEAUX, YOU'VE ALMOST CERTAINLY DRUNK SOME SÉMILLON, SINCE THE REGION'S WHITES ARE USUALLY A BLEND OF THE LATTER AND SAUVIGNON BLANC.

sémillon

It's a good combination. If Sauvignon is all bones and energy, Sémillon is fatter, rounder and more comfortable, adding lovely rich, figgy, honeyed tones to Sauvignon's peppy aromatics.

Sounds good, you might think, so why don't they make a hundred per cent Sémillon? Well, they do in Australia, and when they're not over-oaking it the grape shows really well. With its attractive round mouth-feel, it's a good substitute for Chardonnay and can be drunk happily on its own or with food.

In Sauternes, it's also responsible for some of the world's finest dessert wine, of which more later…

chenin blanc

POOR CHENIN BLANC.
PLANTED IN HUGE NUMBERS
ALL OVER THE WORLD, YET
SO RARELY TALKED ABOUT.
WHY? BECAUSE, TO PUT IT
BLUNTLY, MOST OF WHAT IT
MAKES IS RUBBISH.

Not that this is the fault of the grape itself, oh no. In its purest form, Chenin Blanc can make some of the most intriguing wines in the world. Try a Vouvray or a Savennières from the central Loire Valley in France and you'll find something that is intriguing, challenging and (often) amazing value for money.

But in the past, in places like the US and South Africa it's been used just as a workhorse to give lots of juice for cheap wine or brandy. Happily this is changing, and there are more good examples from these countries, especially South Africa.

GEWÜRZTRAMINER IS A MOUTHFUL IN EVERY SENSE OF THE WORD. ONCE MEMORABLY DESCRIBED BY A THIRSTY CUSTOMER AT A WINERY IN AUSTRALIA AS 'GEE-WHIZZ TRAM-DRIVER', NO WONDER IT'S USUALLY SHORTENED TO GEWÜRZ (PRONOUNCED 'GA-VURTS').

gewürztraminer

The name (which means 'spicy Traminer') might be German, and the grape might be found there, but its heartland is Alsace, at France's eastern edge. It makes powerfully aromatic wines, whose flavours don't so much float out of the glass as hang above it in a dense, perfumed cloud: lychees, roses and Turkish delight are absolutely typical and make it the most recognizable grape varietal in the world. Its big flavours make it a good wine to sip on its own, but it's also your best bet to accompany heavily flavoured Chinese or Thai food.

viognier

IS RED THE NEW BLACK? IS
MONDAY THE NEW FRIDAY?
AND COULD VIOGNIER BE
THE NEW CHARDONNAY?
CERTAINLY, IT'S A GRAPE
THAT'S BECOMING MORE
AND MORE FASHIONABLE,
FOLLOWING ITS SMALL-TOWN
BEGINNINGS IN FRANCE'S
NORTHERN RHÔNE VALLEY.

Now the little country girl has travelled all over the world, and is starting to attract the attention of the wine industry's bigwigs, who think that she might just have star potential.

When she learns her lines and puts her heart into the performance, Viognier gives rich, heady, apricot-flavoured wines that are to die for.

But give her a bad script in an unprepossessing location and her performances are wooden and flat, with little flavour.

Still, there are ever more good examples from places as far apart as the south of France, California, Chile and New Zealand. A future Oscar winner?

fizz

IS THERE ANYONE OUT
THERE WHO DOESN'T LIKE
SPARKLING WINE? FIZZ CAN
TURN A PICNIC INTO AN
OCCASION, A PRE-DINNER
DRINK INTO A CELEBRATION.
IT'S AS CHEERFUL AS A
YOUNG PUPPY, AND WE
LOVE IT FOR ITS OPTIMISM.

The best (and most expensive)
sparklers in the world come from
Champagne – which isn't to say that
every bottle bearing that famous name
comes from this chilly region of north-
eastern France. Plenty of countries
outside Europe use the term as a
catch-all term for anything with bubbles,
and they're rarely as good as the
genuine stuff, so be careful.

There are probably four key elements to good champagne. First, it's made with the right grape varieties, which means Chardonnay, Pinot Noir and Pinot Meunier. And yes, in case you were wondering, the last two are red.

Second, it has decent weight, but also a lovely fresh acidity that keeps the drink light and lively in the mouth. Third, it spends a decent amount of time ageing in the bottle before it is released, which allows the flavours to mellow and mature a bit.

And finally, and perhaps most important, it has great fizz. Really good champagne has a stream of super-fine bubbles. Not fat, lazy ones that expire halfway up your glass, but a vibrant, swaying line of them, rushing to the surface with energy. With champagne, perhaps more than any other drink, you can learn a lot by using your eyes. Non-vintage champagne is a blend of lots of different wines from lots of different years, and is usually 'brut' (dry), meaning it has next to no sugar in it. If you want something a bit sweeter, look for 'demi-sec' (off-dry). Vintage champagne, produced only in the best years, is made just from the grapes of one year. The finest examples can age for decades, taking on amazing complexity with time.

how is champagne made?

There are cheaper, mass-production ways of making sparkling wines, but the classic *méthode champenoise* starts with a fresh,

low-alcohol 'base wine'. Yeast and sugar are then added to the bottle, which starts a second fermentation. As well as raising the alcohol to its final level, this traps the gas in the bottle, producing the fizz (and the pop when you take out the cork).

Rosé champagnes are expensive, luxurious – and vary a lot in quality.

While nowhere else, strictly speaking, makes champagne, other countries make good sparkling wines, with New Zealand (a place with plenty of cool spots like northern France) in the lead.

FIRST OF ALL, RID YOURSELF OF THE IDEA THAT SWEET WINE EQUALS BAD WINE. IT'S TRUE THAT SOME CHEAP AND CHEERFUL WINE STYLES (GERMAN LIEBFRAUMILCH, WHITE ZINFANDEL) ARE PRETTY SUGARY – BUT THAT'S NOT TO SAY THAT ALL SWEET WINES ARE AT THIS UNAMBITIOUS LEVEL.

sweet wines

Indeed, wines like Sauternes and Vouvray (France), Tokaji (Hungary) or the great dessert wines of Italy, Germany and Austria are some of the finest expressions in the world of wine.

Yet for some of the most gorgeous wines on the planet, they aren't much to look at when they're on the vine. In fact, they look more like a disaster that you'd feed the cat than something that wine lovers will be swooning over in a few years' time.

That's due to the rather unattractively named 'noble rot'.

Brought on by warmth and humidity (great sweet-wine areas are nearly all by rivers), it covers the grapes with a downy grey coating that splits the skins and makes the grapes shrivel. OK, they don't look great for the cameras, but

Methods vary, but what all good 'stickies' start with is super-sweet juice that has to be coaxed out of the wizened grapes.

this shrivelling is what allows the grapes to acquire their amazing intensity and concentrate their sugar flavours.

This might give the best sweet wines, but it's not the only way. Some

countries lie unrotted grapes on mats to bake them in the sun like tourists on a sun lounger, while the (red) grapes for Italian Amarone are dried in racks until they shrivel.

So methods vary, but what all good 'stickies' start with is super-sweet juice that has to be coaxed out of the wizened grapes. This, in fact, is why great sweet wines are not cheap. For some wines, you need the fruit of several vines just to make one bottle.

The very best sweet wines may have tooth-rottingly high levels of sugar, but they also have a lovely fresh acidity that means the wine doesn't squat heavily in your mouth like a tin of syrup.

Lighter sweet wines like Muscat or Asti can be a good match with desserts, but super-rich sweeties really require something powerful but savoury such as foie gras, pâté or stinky blue cheese. And, if you're feeling indulgent, you can always just chill it down and sip it on its own, which is the best thing for Germany's greatest stickies.

fortified wines

THERE'S ONLY ONE THING THAT STOPS MOST PEOPLE TRYING
FORTIFIED WINES AND THAT'S PREJUDICE. TOO STRONG, TOO
SWEET, NO GOOD WITH FOOD – NONE OF IT'S TRUE. THE FACT
THAT TERMS LIKE 'PORT' AND 'SHERRY' HAVE OFTEN BEEN
USED IN THE PAST TO DESCRIBE ANY CHEAPO FORTIFIED
DRINK FIT FOR LITTLE MORE THAN COOKING HASN'T HELPED.
THE 'REAL' STUFF, THOUGH, IS CLASSY, ELEGANT, HAS TONS
OF TRADITION AND CAN OFFER GREAT VALUE FOR MONEY.

PORT

Proper port comes only from the baking terraced
vineyards of the Douro Valley in northern Portugal.
Its headquarters is the town of Oporto, hence the
name. It is basically ordinary table wine that has
had a little grape spirit added to it part-way
through the fermentation process. It is sweet,
rich, heady stuff that comes in a variety of styles.

Young ports, like ruby, are cheerful and
inexpensive, good for sipping on their own.
Reserve ports or, better still, late-bottled vintage

(LBV) ports are an affordable way of getting something classy, while aged tawnies or vintage port (expensive) are right at the top of the tree. Majestic wines to be savoured, they are the perfect indulgent partner for cheese.

SHERRY

For starters, let's forget the idea that all sherry is sweet and strong. Most sherries are actually dry and barely above wine strength. Fino (the classic bone-dry white style) is only about fifteen per cent

alcohol – the same as an average Zinfandel. It's great with seafood or as a pre-dinner drink with nibbles, and like all sherries should be served chilled in a decent-sized glass.

Darker sherries like amontillados or olorosos are ideal for drinking on their own, but also good with cold meats, game and soups. The super-sweet, tar-black Pedro Ximénez sherries are good with blue cheeses and ice cream.

MADEIRA

Madeira's big advantage is its ability to stay the same for years after you've opened the bottle. From a tiny volcanic island in the Atlantic off the North African coast, Madeiras are mostly sweet, soft and, with their exotic spicy banana flavours, work well with cakes.

practicalities

garage, or the loft) is a good idea.
swings in temperature will ruin your
in no time, and it's better to keep
mewhere that's a bit too warm, but
ant, than somewhere the
ometer yo-yos.
and store your wine lying down —
s the cork from drying out and
he closure secure.

SERVING

Two main things to get right here:
the glass and the temperature.

When it comes to glasses, the
bigger the better, since they let you
sloosh the wine around a bit, which
frees up the aromas and enhances the
taste. Believe me, paying a bit extra for
a decent set of glasses makes a big
difference to your wine experience.

As does serving your wine at the
right temperature. Whites, obviously,
need to be chilled – but don't go

THE GRAPE GROWERS AND WINEMAKERS HAVE

BIT AND MADE A DECENT BOTTLE OF WINE, BU

ON GETTING THE MOST OUT OF IT IS UP TO YC

BASIC POINTERS ON HOW TO STORE AND SE

PURCHASE CAN MAKE A BIG DIFFERENCE.

storing and se

STORING

If you're planning to drink your wine
within a couple of weeks of buying it, it
doesn't much matter where you keep
it. But since most of us tend to
have bottles of wine hanging around
for a few months (or even years)
before we get round to drinking them,
it helps to get the storage right.

Essentially, wine bottles are like
bats. They don't like heat, light or
being disturbed, which is why cellars

are ideal
you don'
somewh
consta

The
arou
migl
the
Ar
c

overboard. If your wine is too cold it won't taste of anything, so if your fridge is particularly hyperactive take the wine out half an hour before serving, to let it recover a little.

As for reds, the description 'room temperature' is a little misleading. It was coined a hundred years ago, when houses were significantly cooler than they are now – and red wine that's too hot becomes over-alcoholic and unbalanced. So try to keep it somewhere coolish (15°C/59°F is good) before serving.

One last thing: decanting. This is essentially pouring the wine gently from the bottle into another container. It's a way of removing the sediment from old bottles (especially vintage port) or of encouraging a particularly good wine to open out a bit and 'breathe' a couple of hours before serving. If you don't have a fancy decanter, a jug will do just fine.

matching
food and wine

IN A SENSE, ADVISING PEOPLE WHAT WINE TO DRINK WITH
WHAT FOOD IS LIKE TELLING THEM WHAT CLOTHES TO WEAR.
SURE, SOME THINGS WORK BETTER TOGETHER THAN OTHERS,
BUT AT THE END OF THE DAY IT'S ALL ABOUT PERSONAL
CHOICE – AND IF YOU LIKE CABERNET SAUVIGNON WITH ICE
CREAM THEN DON'T LET ANYBODY TELL YOU DIFFERENT.

Having said that, there are some combinations that simply work better than others – and if you're having guests round for a meal they might not share your idiosyncrasies. With more styles of food and wine, from all over the world, more widely available today than ever before, getting a perfect match is probably harder than it was twenty years ago. Yet for all that, it doesn't have to be rocket science, and a few basics will get you a long way.

Most basic of all, to my mind, is weight. Irrespective of flavour profiles, if you manage to get

Irrespective of flavour profiles, if you manage to get the right weight of wine for your food you're off to a good start.

the right weight of wine for your food you're off to a good start. And this really isn't that complicated. Light food needs lighter wine; hearty food needs bigger wine. Easy!

I mean, it stands to reason that if you're having a fragrant, crunchy salad, or some lightly flavoured langoustines, you'll want something equally light to go with them that isn't going to dominate the dish. Likewise, a big fat steak in pepper sauce is going to stamp all over a delicate bottle of Muscadet. See the table on page 57 for a quick guide.

OK, SO YOU'VE DECIDED ON THE *WEIGHT* OF YOUR DISH; NEXT YOU WANT TO LOOK AT WHAT *STYLE* OF FOOD IT IS. FOR INSTANCE, CLASSIC, SIMPLE FOOD WITHOUT ZINGY FLAVOURS – LIKE FILLET STEAK OR ROAST CHICKEN – TENDS TO WORK BEST WITH 'CLASSIC'-STYLE WINES – SAY, A CABERNET OR MERLOT FOR THE FIRST ONE, AND A LIGHTLY OAKED CHARDONNAY FOR THE SECOND.

Simple dishes like these are often the best way to showcase a really special bottle of wine that you've been saving for a special occasion, because they are able to show off their full flavours without any big food tastes getting in the way.

As important as looking at the main ingredient in the dish is what's going on around it – things like sauces and accompaniments, which can, in fact,

be the defining factor in deciding your final wine choice.

Thus, if a food has a big rich gravy with it – or lots of highly flavoured side dishes – you'll need to upgrade your wine size as well. For example, if you're cooking pork (usually a mid-weight red match), but it's going to be served with a creamy sauce, you might want a big white with a bit of acidity to help cut through the richness.

As for less traditional dishes, there's no need to be intimidated. Using the basic information we've got we should be able to find a solution. Thus, sushi (light, unsauced, delicate) works really well with fino sherry, while Chinese food (heavily flavoured, exotic) works

well with heavier Alsace whites such as Gewürztraminer or Pinot Gris.

The only area where you need to be careful is with hot or spicy food. First of all, don't waste an expensive bottle on heavily flavoured, spice-laden food. Secondly, since tannin (in red wines) makes the food taste hotter than it is, don't choose a super-dry red wine. In fact, when it comes to Thai, Indian or Malay curries, don't be afraid to match white wines with red meat, since the extra acidity freshens your mouth and counteracts the heat.

For Mexican food, find a sweetly juicy red without too much tannin – maybe a spicy Shiraz.

HINT

Don't forget that the wines that work best with food tend to have a decent structure – tannin for red wines and acidity for whites. Soft, fruity wines that work well on their own in front of the telly might not be able to stand up to the weight of food.

watch your weight

The table below obviously isn't comprehensive, because so much depends on the producer, the region and even the vintage. That's why Chardonnay, for instance, can veer from light and wispy to big and chunky. But it's a good starting point and will help you out to begin with.

LIGHT WHITES
Muscadet, Sauvignon Blanc, Soave, Riesling, fino sherry, champagne

LIGHT REDS
Beaujolais, Valpolicella, Barbera

MEDIUM WHITES
Unoaked Chardonnay, Chenin Blanc, Viognier, Pinot Gris, Pinot Blanc

MEDIUM REDS
Pinot Noir/Burgundy, Rioja, Chianti, Merlot, young Bordeaux, Mediterranean reds, Primitivo, Malbec, Pinotage, some Zinfandel

HEAVYWEIGHT WHITES
Oaked Chardonnay, top Burgundy, old-style white Rioja, Alsace Gewürztraminer

HEAVYWEIGHT REDS
Expensive Cabernet Sauvignon, Californian Merlot, old Bordeaux, top Rhône reds, Australian Shiraz, Barolo/Barbaresco, some Zinfandel, Châteauneuf-du-Pape

ordering wine

IT MIGHT NOT BE UP THERE WITH MOVING HOUSE AND DIVORCE, BUT ORDERING WINE IN A RESTAURANT CAN BE AN ARTERY-STRAINING EXPERIENCE. GET THE WINES RIGHT AND EVEN AN AVERAGE MEAL BECOMES A FIVE-STAR EXPERIENCE; GET THEM WRONG AND NEVER MIND THE FOOD, YOU WON'T BE FLAVOUR OF THE MONTH EITHER. HERE ARE A FEW TIPS TO MAKE SURE YOU GET IT RIGHT MORE OFTEN THAN NOT.

WORK OUT WHAT EVERYONE IS EATING

This might sound obvious – but there's no point in ordering bottles of full-bodied Cabernet Sauvignon if everyone is eating fish. Unless, of course, your group happens to like fish and red wine.

CHECK OUT WINES BY THE GLASS

Wines by the glass are a brilliant addition to wine lists – and are thankfully growing in popularity. Aside from allowing everyone to order something different to match their food, they can be a good way of checking out a bottle that you quite fancy, but aren't a hundred per cent sure about. Try it by the glass with your starter, then order a full bottle for the group with your mains. Also, if three out of your party are eating meat and one is having seafood, then a judicious single-glass purchase keeps everyone happy.

USE YOUR WAITER

Having a waiter (or wine waiter, if you're lucky) working for you can take a lot of the stress out of ordering wine. He should know both the food menu and the wine list, and, if you give instructions as precisely as you can regarding style and price, ought to be able to find a good match. Whatever you do, don't feel embarrassed about asking – and don't allow them to talk you into paying more than you want to.

LOOK FOR CLUES ON THE WINE LIST

Nowadays more and more wine lists have helpful descriptions of the flavours of the wines and even, in some cases, food-matching suggestions. Make the most of them.

IF ABROAD, DRINK LOCALLY WHEREVER POSSIBLE

OK, so it might not be possible in Sweden or Russia, but if the place you're visiting has a significant wine industry of its own, you should check it out. For starters, the locals will be flattered and will want to show off what their area is capable of, so you should get a good recommendation, but it will probably also be cheaper.

AVOID HOUSE WINES

Yes, really. House wines are massively marked up and rarely deliver good value for money. For an extra ten or twenty per cent more you'll almost certainly get twice as good a wine.

CHEAP DOESN'T ALWAYS MEAN CHEERFUL

Restaurant mark-ups are brutal. Accept that you will probably have to spend at least three times as much as you would for a bottle to drink at home and start looking around that level.

GO FOR NAMES YOU KNOW

Eating out can be a good opportunity to try wines that you wouldn't normally consider. But if you are really terrified of getting a turkey, look for a few brand names that you know and trust.

LOOK FOR GOOD VINTAGES

Nobody can be expected to remember all the good vintages from all over the world. But there are certain times when you can pick almost any producer from a region and the year was so good that the wine is likely to be fantastic.

Examples are Bordeaux 2000 and Chianti 1997. Then, to make life easier, 2001 seems to have been a fantastic year in a whole load of places. You should do OK with 2001s from the Rhône, Rioja, California, Chile and Australia – and there should be plenty of these wines about.

THE BALE-OUT

If you are really struggling, certain wine styles make good 'bale-outs' – not necessarily the best wines on the list, but solid and reliable: Chilean Cabernet Sauvignon, Californian Merlot, Australian Chardonnay and Shiraz, South African Chenin Blanc (if not too cheap), Italian Primitivo, New Zealand Sauvignon Blanc.

AND FINALLY

The key thing when ordering wine is not to get too uptight about it. It is, after all, only a part of the whole experience and shouldn't spoil a night out. If you order a wine that you really don't like, see if the restaurant will replace it (some will even if there's nothing actually wrong with the wine). Failing that, it's not as if you have to live with the decision for the whole of your life. Everyone makes mistakes with the wine list – even experts. The nice thing about wine is that you can always buy another bottle...

wine words

ACIDITY

An essential element of whites and (to a lesser extent) red wines, adding freshness.

APPELLATION

A specially marked out region that defines the limits of where it's possible to produce a particular style of wine. Bordeaux, Chianti, Champagne, Napa Valley and Burgundy are all *appellations*, for instance.

BALANCE

The way a wine's fruit flavours, structure and alcohol levels interact. If one of the three dominates, the wine is out of balance.

CLARET

Another name for red Bordeaux – though some places have hijacked the name to mean generic red wine.

CORK TAINT/CORKED

Nothing to do with having bits of cork floating in your wine. It's when the cork is infected with a pungent bacteria, which transfers its aroma to the wine. Distinguished by a horrible, mushroomy flavour.

D.O.

A Spanish name for an *appellation*. Stands for *Denominación de Origen*.

DRY

A wine that has no sugar left in it.

FERMENTATION

The process that turns sugar (in grapes) into alcohol. The more sugar there is in a grape when it's picked, the higher the potential alcohol.

FINISH

The intensity of flavours left in your mouth once you've swallowed the wine. Some finishes can last for minutes!

GRAPE VARIETAL/VARIETY

The type of grape used to make the wine. Cabernet Sauvignon, Chardonnay and Merlot are all grape varietals or grape varieties.

MERITAGE

American name for a red wine made with a blend of the classic Bordeaux grapes, Cabernet Sauvignon, Merlot and Cabernet Franc (plus, sometimes, Petit Verdot).

OAK

Wines (red and white) often spend time ageing in oak barrels, which adds a spicy, toasty or vanilla flavour.

STRUCTURE

Tannin and acidity provide the skeleton on which a wine's fruit flavours hang. Without them, it just tastes like grape juice.

TANNIN

An essential component of red wines, providing structure. If your teeth feel dry once you've swallowed, that's tannin.

TERROIR

Untranslatable French word meaning the combination of geography, climate and soil that go to make a place's wines taste as they do.

WINE WEBSITES

www.champagnemagic.com
 The champagne enthusiast's website,
 with a comprehensive list of producers.

www.decanter.com
www.winespectator.com
 The online versions of the top British
 and American wine magazines.

www.winecountry.com
 A comprehensive guide to touring
 the wine regions of California.

www.wine-lovers-page.com
 An independent wine appreciation
 site for beginners and experienced
 enthusiasts alike.

www.wine-pages.com
 Articles and features, including
 a DIY wine appreciation course.

PICTURE CREDITS

All photographs by Alan Williams except:

Francesca Yorke pages 6 right, 12 below
 right, 21, 33 below, 39, 51
Peter Cassidy pages 40, 41
Debi Treloar pages 15 above left, 53
William Lingwood page 45 right